Contents

Battle with gravity **4**

What is mountain biking? **6**

Getting started **8**

Starting to race **10**

Parts of a bike **12**

Biking equipment **14**

Bike set-up **16**

Riding style **18**

Technique **20**

Mountain bike muscle **22**

Mountain bike training **24**

Cross training **26**

Eating for fitness **28**

Racing fuel **30**

Support crew **32**

The biking year **34**

Race preparation **36**

Racing tactics **38**

Big competitions **40**

Pro rider **42**

World and Olympic champions **44**

Glossary **46**

Resources **47**

Index **48**

Words printed in bold letters, **like these**, are explained in the Glossary.

Battle with gravity

One of the most exciting mountain bike events is the downhill. As with ski racing, the riders go one after another down a pre-set course. The winner is whoever gets to the bottom in the quickest time. The 2003 women's world championship downhill event saw a classic battle between the most successful racer ever, France's Anne-Caroline Chausson, and the world's other top racers.

Hot competition

Anne-Caroline Chausson was the racer all the other riders feared most, and the red-hot favourite to win. She was world BMX champion in 1993, world downhill junior champion from 1993–95, and world champion for six years from 1996 to 2002. Victory would bring 'Anne-Caro' yet another world downhill championship to add to her already impressive collection of titles.

However, some of the world's best riders were also in the field, desperate to end Anne-Caro's winning run. Fionn Griffiths and Tracey Moseley of the UK, second and third in the 2002 championships, were there. So too were Kathy Pruitt and Marla Streb of the USA, and Sabrina Jonnier and Nolvenn Le Caer of France, Anne-Caro's teammates. The stage was set for one of the most thrilling downhill races for years.

Marla Streb in full body armour on the World Cup downhill course at Lugano, Switzerland in 2003. Competitors found the steep, rocky course very demanding, and needed to be fit and strong to finish in a fast time.

The course

The competition, at Lugano in Switzerland, was held over a steep, technically challenging 1-kilometre (1.45 mile) course. As 2003 US champion Marla Streb said, 'Most people made mistakes on the course because of their hands and arms being so tired... those that had the most relaxed hands throughout the run [were] able to ride the bottom of the course clean.' The rider who used least energy on the demanding upper part of the course was probably going to win.

Many riders struggled with the challenges posed by the tricky route, which needed a combination of skill and strength through its tight turns and rocky sections. But late in the competition Tracey Moseley of the UK posted a fast time of 5:33.31. With only eight riders to go, Moseley was in the lead and looking good for a medal.

But then came the French women's team assault on the course. First Nolvenn Le Caer posted a faster time; then Sabrina Jonnier pushed Moseley into third. Finally, Anne-Caro launched herself down the course. Riding at a different level from the others, she sliced huge chunks of time from her competitors. Her final time of 5:10.23 was a massive 12 seconds faster than silver medallist Jonnier.

Anne-Caroline Chausson

Nickname:	'Anne-Caro'
Born:	1977 at Dijon, France
Hometown:	La Massana, Andorra
Height:	172 cm
Weight:	59 kg
Hobbies:	Free skiing, BMX, travelling
Favourite food:	Seafood
Drink:	Fresh juice
Dislikes:	Soccer, chocolate cake, snakes, people too proud of themselves, guns

Anne-Caroline is the most successful mountain biker ever. By the age of 23 she had won more World Cup races in a single discipline (downhill) than any other rider.

What is mountain biking?

Mountain biking first started in California in the USA during the 1970s. A bunch of friends would get together and race modified **beach cruisers** downhill. When they reached the bottom, they would throw the bikes in the back of a pick-up truck, drive back up the hill, and do it again. From this small beginning, mountain biking has grown into an Olympic sport.

Cross-country

Cross-country racing is the type of mountain biking that has featured in the Olympics since 1996. The riders compete over a circular course, riding lightweight bikes. Cross-country courses differ from place to place. Some courses are relatively flat and smooth, which suits riders who are good at riding at a constant high speed. Other courses are bumpier and more hilly: these suit riders who enjoy varying their speed and have good techniques for dealing with difficult obstacles.

Dual slalom and 4x

In dual slalom competitions, two riders at a time race down a course side by side, through specially built jumps and turns. The winner goes through to the next round, and the racing continues until one rider is crowned champion. Recently a similar type of racing called **4x** has become popular. It features four riders instead of two.

Women's racing is every bit as tough as the men's competitions, with very high skill levels – as this shot of a 4x race shows!

Downhill

In downhill racing the riders race one after another down a seemingly impossible route. They perform jumps and slides as they look for the fastest way down the course. **Full-face helmets** and **body armour** are crucial, as the spectacular crashes can be very dangerous. The rider who gets down the hill fastest wins.

Endurance racing

Over the last few years, the number of endurance races has increased dramatically. In these, teams of riders race over a set time period, usually 24 hours. They ride one at a time, as a relay team. The challenge is to go further in 24 hours than any other team can manage.

Endurance events test riders and their equipment to the limit. Often there are mechanics and masseurs on hand to tend to damaged bikes and aching riders.

Thomas Frischknecht

Nickname: 'Frischi'
Born: February 1970
Home: Feldbach, Switzerland
Occupation: Professional cyclist
                  since 1990
Height: 176 cm
Weight: 67 kg
Favourite music: U2
Favourite food: Sushi

'Frischi' is a legendary rider. He was a world junior **cyclo-cross** champion and also races on the road. By the end of 2003 he had totted up nine mountain biking world championships, seventeen World Cup race victories, a European Championship, a second place in the 1996 Olympics in Atlanta, USA and a sixth place in the 2000 Olympics in Sydney, Australia.

Getting started

It can be easy to get carried away with all the expensive bikes and equipment that are available for mountain biking. But most top riders started their careers on cheap, simple bikes and only moved on to expensive gear later. The very first 'mountain bikers', after all, rode **beach cruiser** bikes, which are not even what we think of as 'proper' mountain bikes today.

Matching the terrain

Top riders choose different bikes for different competitions. Few ordinary people are this lucky: they just have one bike for every kind of ride. This is fine: most bikes with knobbly tyres (tyres that have shaped knobs on them, rather than being smooth) and a wide range of gears can be used off-road.

It is important, though, that your bike is always strong enough for the job you want it to do. Trying spectacular jumps or extreme downhill routes on a lightweight cross-country bike is likely to result in the bike breaking and the rider suffering injury.

Basic requirements

The basic needs of a mountain biker are very simple. They need a bike that will go off-road, a helmet, some water, suitable clothes (warm if the weather is cold, cool if the weather is hot), a pump and puncture repair kit, and a clear idea of where they're going.

Not everyone rides in the snow! But varying weather and landscapes are one of the attractions of mountain biking.

First ride

Most people first get into mountain biking when a friend persuades them to come along on a ride. Often this first ride turns out to be surprisingly hard work. People who have only ever ridden a bike on the road find off-road riding a lot tougher than they expect – the bike slips and slides around, and the rough ground makes it hard to keep an even pedalling speed.

What usually persuades people to have a second try at mountain biking is the speed and excitement of the sport. Racing your friends up a hill, lungs bursting from the effort, then careering down the other side, hanging on to the brakes to slow down, is very exciting.

Ride planning

It is important that everyone on a ride knows where they are going and how to get back. Experienced bikers often build in an 'escape route' – a way of shortening the ride if it is taking too long or someone gets too tired to finish the full route. It is also important to know how to repair a puncture, as these can be common!

Puncture facts

- Special mountain-bike tyres and inner tubes are available that are more puncture-resistant than normal bicycle ones.
- Some racers carry gas canisters that allow them to reinflate their tyres at super-quick speeds.

One thing all mountain bikers get to learn sooner or later is how to mend a puncture! It is good to practise this skill: having to mend a puncture for the first time in a race would be a disaster.

Starting to race

Racers like Sue Thomas, the top British cross-country rider in 2003, or Nathan Rennie of Australia, the World Cup downhill winner, were not always at the top of their sport. A few years ago they were just ordinary kids who were interested in cycling. So, how did they end up as leading members of their national mountain bike teams?

Early races

People get into mountain-bike racing in lots of different ways. Some start by entering a race for a dare. Others might come from a BMX, road racing or even **motocross** background. Wherever they come from, a few people finish their first race and promptly decide never to do another one! But many are gripped by the competition experience and become determined to do better next time. This is usually when they consider joining a club.

Joining a club

Most riders discover their local club through their national cycling organization. Often these have websites with club details or they can give advice by phone. Joining a mountain-bike club has several advantages for newcomers to racing. Most important, they get access to a qualified cycling coach. (One sign that a club is a good one is that it has at least one qualified coach.) Coaches will be able to give advice on training and technique, as well as the best tactics for racing.

If a racer starts to do very well in competitions – perhaps coming in the top three in most events – they might be asked to represent their region in national competitions. If they continue to win, they may even get to join the national team. At this level, racers usually get support from the national organization. This usually means help with training and coaching, and probably also some financial support.

Coaches play a big part in the careers of most top riders. Britain's Sue Thomas, shown here racing in 2003, was once asked who had most influenced her riding. She replied: 'My old coach – I worked with Martin Early for about 4 years... he's been a massive influence.'

Talent spotting

Most national cycling organizations also have talent scouts out looking for young people who could become great cyclists. In Britain, for example, British Cycling has a system for young people to come along and be tested for cycling talent, even if they do not cycle at the moment. If they then pass a series of physical tests, the organization offers them help to become a racing cyclist.

Riders like this gain excellent experience of the racing scene by starting young on the competition circuit.

Roland Green

Born: July 1974
Lives: Victoria, BC, Canada
Height: 180 cm
Weight: 73 kg
Honours: Cross-country 2001 and 2002 World Champion; 2001 World Cup series winner and National Off-Road Bicycle Association (NORBA) winner.

Roland's cycling career started because he wanted a few extra minutes in bed before school! He would let the school bus go then race after it on his bike. Throughout his career, Roland has had to overcome the challenge of a serious allergy to pollen. This made racing in the spring and early summer extremely difficult.

Roland Green makes pre-race preparations. The earpiece will keep him in contact with his team manager, who gives advice on when to attack.

Parts of a bike

The bikes used by top riders like 2001 world champion Alison Dunlap of the USA are complex pieces of engineering wizardry. Unbelievably light, they weigh as little as 8.5 kilograms and cost thousands of pounds. The advanced technology that goes into bikes like Alison's trickles down through every manufacturer's range. Even their least expensive mountain bikes will be suitable for off-road riding and racing.

Frames

The frame is the heart of every mountain bike. It has to be stiff enough not to bend as the rider puts pressure through the pedals. It also has to be light enough to make pedalling easy, but strong enough not to break. Cross-country frames do not need to be as strong as downhill or dual slalom frames. For this reason, they often have thinner tubes to reduce weight.

Wheels and tyres

As well as light frames, cross-country racers use wheels with lightweight **rims** and tyres and a reduced number of **spokes**. Downhill racers have **gravity** on their side helping them speed downhill, so they rarely worry about wheel weight. For them, it is important that the wheel is strong enough to withstand the bangs it will receive on the way to the finish.

Position facts

Cross-country bikes usually have the saddle at about the same height as the handlebars, to give a more aerodynamic, powerful pedalling position. Downhill bikes have the saddle set much lower: the rider doesn't need to pedal much, but will need to keep his or her weight further back to avoid tipping over the handlebars.

Christopher Kovarik of Australia is pictured here aboard a typical downhill bike. He has shifted his weight way back, with his bottom out behind the saddle, to balance the bike on the steep downhill slope. Otherwise he would be at risk of going over the handlebars.

Handlebars

Cross-country bikes use flat or nearly flat handlebars, to help the rider keep an **aerodynamic** position. Downhill bikes tend to have wider, higher bars to give the rider a more 'upright' riding position. That way they can see more easily the obstacles that lie ahead.

Groupset

'Groupset' is the name given to all the other components that make up a bike: the brakes, gears and so on. Some are lighter than others, but generally all groupsets made by big manufacturers tend to work well.

saddle

triple **chainset** with three rings on the front

V-brakes, which work by holding a rubber pad on the wheel rim

seat tube

top tube

down tube

head tube

eight, nine or ten-speed rear **cog**

rear brakes

clipless pedal – this attaches to a '**cleat**' on the bottom of a rider's shoe

front suspension – cross-country riders normally just have front suspension with about 60–80 mm movement, to soak up the worst vibrations from the trail.

This is a typical cross-country bike. Although some bikes are more expensive than others, all share the same basic features.

Biking equipment

Mountain bike racers have to be ready to train and compete in all kinds of weather and conditions. The 2004 Olympics took place in the searing heat of a Greek summer, and it is a safe bet that the gold-medal winners there would have done their pre-championship training in similar conditions. But races are held all round the world, from the tropical heat of Cairns in Australia to the chilly air of the Swiss Alps in springtime – so it is important always to be prepared.

Summer biking gear

Essential summer biking gear includes:
- Lycra shorts with padded insert to improve comfort.
- A cycling top with long zip for ventilation.
- Shoes with mesh tops for ventilation.
- Lightweight, fingerless gloves to improve comfort for hands.

Winter biking gear

Essential winter biking gear includes:
- Thermal tights worn over shorts, or alone if padded.
- A thermal base layer.
- A fleece.
- A jacket with a windproof front to reduce cold. Extra layers can be added as the cold increases.
- Winter shoes with neoprene cuffs to keep out water and mud.
- Padded, windproof fleece gloves to keep fingers warm.

Clothing

Most riders avoid wearing anything too flappy on a bike. Clothes that are reasonably close-fitting are best, because they offer less wind resistance and are unlikely to get caught in a bike's moving parts.

Tools

Most riders carry a small tool kit with them. As a minimum, racers would normally carry:

- a mini-tool with a selection of allen keys (l-shaped tools for tightening and loosening bolts), a small flat-head screwdriver and one or two spanners (wrenches)
- a chain splitter (a device that allows them to repair a broken chain)
- a puncture repair kit or instant patches
- a bicycle pump to reinflate tyres.

This mini toolkit would be a vital piece of equipment for all serious mountain bikers.

Hydration

It is vitally important that top-level athletes keep **hydrated** during a race. This means they need to drink plenty of water, or even better a special drink that will help replace the salts and other **nutrients** they are using up. Most riders carry their drink in a water bottle held in a cage on the frame. Others prefer to wear a backpack with a special water container. This allows the rider to suck drink through a tube from the pack while the race is in progress, without taking their hands from the handlebars. The packs can also be used to carry tools and spare clothes.

Safety gear

All racers are required to wear a helmet. Almost everyone wears a helmet whenever they go out on a mountain bike. In the past, helmets were uncomfortable and sweaty, but today they are light and comfortable to wear, with excellent ventilation.

Downhill racers take protection even more seriously than cross-country riders. This is probably no surprise, considering that they travel downhill at speeds of over 60 kilometres (40 miles) per hour. Downhillers wear **full-face helmets** and **body armour** to protect themselves if they crash.

Bike set-up

To ride a mountain bike as fast as possible, it has to be set up properly to fit the rider. Professional racers like Filip Meirhaeghe of Belgium are quite likely to have their bikes specially made, with the frame providing an exact fit to the length of their legs, body and arms. But any bike can usually be adjusted to give the rider a little extra speed.

Biomechanical efficiency

The aim when setting up a bike is to allow the rider to squeeze the maximum efficiency possible from their pedalling. Their position on the bike needs to mix **aerodynamic** shape with comfort. If a rider is too hunched over they will not be able to breathe properly or see obstacles on their route. If they are positioned too upright they will be held back by extra wind resistance.

Filip Meirhaeghe, one of the world's top mountain-bike racers, sprints across the finish line at the end of one of the 2003 World Cup cross-country races.

Frame fact

On a mountain bike, the frame has a sloping top tube to avoid accidents where the rider gets injured on the top tube. Most riders aim to have about a 80–100 mm gap between the top tube and their crotch while standing on the floor.

Saddle height and position

Many riders first set their saddle height by sitting on the bike in their bike shoes, with their heel on the pedal. The saddle is the right height if their knee is very slightly bent when the pedal is at the bottom of its revolution (turn). If the rider's hips rock from side to side once they start pedalling, they know the saddle is set too high and may cause an injury. They must lower it a couple of millimetres.

Saddle position is set using a **plumb line**. Riders move the saddle back and forth until a plumb line dangling from just behind their kneecap goes straight through the pedal spindle, when the **crank** is parallel to the ground.

Cleats

Riders using clipless pedals normally set their shoe **cleats** so that the pedal spindle is under the ball of their foot.

Stem and handlebars

The last adjustment riders make is their 'reach' to the handlebars. Many use a common rule of thumb, which says that if the **axle** of the front wheel is hidden from view behind the handlebars, the 'reach' is right. If the axle is behind the bars, a shorter stem may be needed. If it were in front, a longer stem would provide a more aerodynamic position.

This diagram shows how to make sure a bike's saddle and handlebars are set at the correct height.

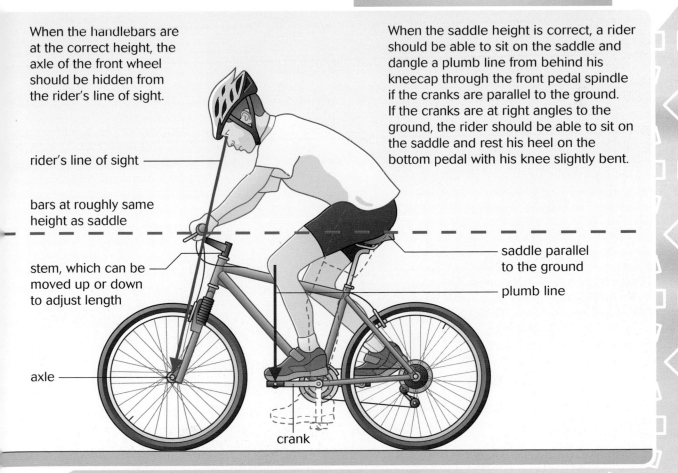

When the handlebars are at the correct height, the axle of the front wheel should be hidden from the rider's line of sight.

When the saddle height is correct, a rider should be able to sit on the saddle and dangle a plumb line from behind his kneecap through the front pedal spindle if the cranks are parallel to the ground. If the cranks are at right angles to the ground, the rider should be able to sit on the saddle and rest his heel on the bottom pedal with his knee slightly bent.

rider's line of sight

bars at roughly same height as saddle

stem, which can be moved up or down to adjust length

axle

saddle parallel to the ground

plumb line

crank

Riding style

Race commentators often mention that a particular rider has their own 'style', but what does this mean? 'Riding style' sums up several factors: the racer's position on the bike, their pedalling action and how they hold their head are some of the main ones. Most top-level cyclists aim to have as smooth a style as possible, channelling all their energy into their pedal power.

Cadence and gears

The speed at which a rider turns the pedals (and therefore the gear they select) is known as their 'cadence'. The right cadence is affected by conditions: riding into the wind may require a higher cadence and an easier gear than riding with the wind behind you,

for example. Generally, though, most riders are comfortable at a cadence of 70 to 80 rpm (revolutions per minute), which is just more than one pedal revolution per second. The most experienced racers may have a higher cadence, of 80 to 90 rpm.

Christof Sauser of Switzerland shows good uphill technique: elbows bent and weight forward to keep the front wheel from lifting as he drives ahead. He will be keeping the bike in a gear where he is pushing hard, but still able to keep the pedals spinning. Once the pedal strokes become too slow, it is very easy to lose speed.

Climbing hills

Inexperienced mountain-bike riders often try to ride uphill staying in the same gear, and end up having to stand up on the pedals, rocking the bike from side to side and using their upper body to add power. Over a long climb this is exhausting. Standing up like this also takes weight off the back wheel, making it more likely to slip on any loose ground.

Top racers like Mary Grigson, a five-times Australian national champion (1998–2002), select an easier gear to ride uphill. This allows them to keep a higher cadence, which has two main advantages. First, they can stay in the saddle, which drains much less energy than standing up on the pedals. Second, a higher cadence allows them to ride up sudden increases in the slope much more easily.

Shifting fact

Top cross-country racers aim to keep their cadence steady on hills. They do this by shifting gears early, before their cadence starts to drop.

Gunn-Rita Dahle

Born: February 1973
Nationality: Norwegian
Years riding: 8
Height: 173 cm
Weight: 64 kg
Hobbies: Looking after kittens, hiking and reading

Gunn-Rita was world and European cross-country champion in 2002, and has been one of the best bikers around since 1996. She has won many World Cup races, and is also a good road racer, having won one of the stages in the 1998 women's Tour de France.

Technique

Good uphill riding technique is one of the keys to successful cross-country riding. Downhill racers, though, develop a different set of skills – skills that help them descend very fast. Of course, downhill riding techniques are used in cross-country too, but in downhill the bikes are stronger and heavier, the slopes steeper and the racing more extreme.

Taking a line

Expert downhillers like Steve Peat of England make sure they know every centimetre of the course before a competition. They pick the best 'line' – the smoothest, fastest way through each turn. Then they focus on where they want to go, relaxing their body and allowing it automatically to steer the bike in the right direction.

One mistake newcomers to the sport often make is to look at the ground in front of their wheel, trying to spot small obstacles like stones. The bike will usually flow over these anyway, and looking down like this increases the feeling of speed, and therefore fear. This makes the rider tense up, which in turn increases the likelihood of a crash.

Obstacle fact

Never look at an obstacle you want to avoid (experts call this 'hazard fixation') or you are almost certain to hit it! Instead, look where you want to go, and the bike should follow.

Steve Peat of England, world downhill champion in 2002, picks his line through a rocky course in Orgiva, Spain. He lets the front wheel lift away from the rock and keeps his weight back, trusting the bike's suspension to deal with the landing.

Grip through turns

Top riders use two key techniques to get the maximum grip through turns.

1 They look 'through' the turn, at the point where the two sides of the trail come together – this is known as the 'vanishing point'. Racers use the vanishing point to judge speed: if it is coming towards them, the turn is getting tighter and they slow down. If the vanishing point is getting further away, the turn is straightening and they accelerate.

2 Racers try to keep their weight balanced, with enough pressure on the front tyre to allow it to grip. If the back wheel slides it may not be disastrous, but if the front wheel slips out, their race will probably be over.

This rider shows good downhill technique. His weight is towards the back of the bike to give clear vision ahead and ensure that he does not tip forward over the handlebars. His knees and elbows are bent to help absorb shocks.

Tinker Juarez

Born: March 1961
Height: 173 cm
Weight: 63 kg
Hometown: Downey, California, USA

Tinker Juarez's career highlights include being a US Olympic team member (1996, 2000), being a three-time NORBA National Cross-Country Champion (1994, 1995 and 1998), and winning a silver medal at the 1994 World Cross-Country Championships. Tinker's trademark dreadlocks make him one of the sport's most recognizable figures.

Mountain bike muscle

It seems obvious that mountain bikers need to have strength in their legs, and of course they do. But top racers make sure their whole body is fit, including their upper body, which they use to steer their bike over rough ground. Strength and flexibility in their abdomen and lower back also help racers keep an efficient position on the bike.

Endurance and strength

Top-level mountain bikers need to train for two different kinds of fitness: endurance and strength. Endurance, also known as **aerobic** fitness, is the ability to keep your muscles working efficiently over a long period of time. Mountain bikers taking part in a 2-hour cross-country race, or a 24-hour endurance event, find their fitness is pushed to the limit. Kilometre after kilometre, they will be trying to balance their speed against the distance they have to travel, making sure their muscles do not use up all their energy before the finish.

These members of a race squad are out training together. Once one of them stands up on the pedals and sprints for the top of the hill, pride says they all have to! But standing up in this way burns a lot of energy, and is a technique that is best used sparingly.

Often several racers get close to the finish line at the same time. This is where the second type of fitness, strength, comes in. The riders must sprint for the finish, powering to the line in an attempt to grab victory. The contest is no longer about aerobic fitness. With such a short way to go, it becomes a battle to see whose legs are strong enough to hurtle them forward quickest.

Training

The best way to get fit for riding a bike is to ride a bike. Specific mountain bike training techniques include heart-rate training and keeping a training diary (see pages 24–25). Many riders also like to combine biking with other types of fitness activity, which makes the training less boring. This is known as 'cross-training' (see pages 26–27).

Strength training fact

Many top riders use weight training as a way of building their strength. Normally they use weight training during the **off-season**, since, as one top coach says, 'strength training and cycling don't mix well when done [together]'. Cyclists work on their shoulders and neck, chest, arms, back and abdominal muscles, since these can help when riding the bike in a sprint. Racers also work on their leg strength using weights.

Lack of training can lead to the humiliation of having to push your bike uphill!

Top US rider Brian Lopes during weight training. Weights like these are known as 'free weights'. Most riders no longer use free weights. Instead they use weight machines, which control the movement of the weights and make injuries less likely.

Mountain bike training

Today, top cyclists in most disciplines take a very scientific view of training. Their bodies are seen almost as machines, and great care is taken to make sure they work as well as possible. To do this, the best riders have to do the right amount and degree of training at the correct time.

Heart-rate training

Most top cyclists use a heart-rate monitor as part of their training. This is a portable device that measures the speed at which the rider's heart is beating. Most racers work out their maximum heart rate (MHR) by taking their age away from 220. So the maximum heart rate for a 16-year-old rider would be about 204. If their training programme calls for heavy work to increase power and fitness, cyclists aim for a high heart rate – perhaps 85 per cent of their maximum. Then, to help their body recover quickly from this hard work, they keep their heart rate low for the next few rides – perhaps to 60 per cent of their maximum.

Keeping a training diary

All coaches encourage racers to keep a training diary to record what they have done in training and compare it to their plans. For instance, in a week where they expected to cover 120 kilometres, did they manage it, and was it done at the right heart rate? Over the years the diary also allows a racer to work out which types of training get them the best results.

Barrie Clarke, one of Britain's most consistent bike racers, trains hard using a heart-rate monitor. This allows him to work out the effect his training will have on his fitness and speed.

Overtraining

One of the worst things any biker can do is to overtrain and not allow their body time to recover from the work it has done. The effects of this can be drastic. For example, when Canadian cyclist Peter Reid increased his training with an extra 8 hours of cycling, his performances suffered terribly. Reid failed to finish almost all his races in 2001 and 2002. Things only improved after he took a break and began to include two rest days a week in his training routine.

Building rest periods into training schedules is vital, but these do not have to be days without exercise. A ride at 60 per cent of MHR actually helps riders recover more quickly than complete rest. It increases blood flow, makes **nutrients** circulate more quickly and reduces muscle soreness.

It can be tempting to simply get out and ride as often as possible, especially on a sunny day. But top riders plan their training carefully, and use a diary to record exactly what they've done.

Heart-rate facts

This table shows the percentage of a rider's maximum heart rate (MHR) he or she should aim for in certain circumstances.

Percentage of MHR:	Description:
60–65	Easy riding; recovery
65–70	Endurance base training
70–80	**Aerobic capacity** training
80–85	**Lactate threshold** training
85+	Maximum **aerobic** training

Cross training

Many riders try to vary their bike training, choosing to add other activities to their schedule. This is a good way of increasing their general fitness. It also makes it less likely that the training will become too boring!

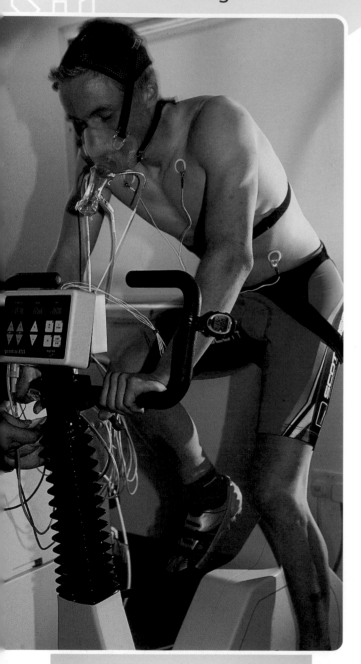

This professional racer looks like a mad scientist's experiment! In fact he is being tested at the Renault Formula 1 Performance Centre, England.

SRM testing

To measure their progress in training, many top riders hook up to a device known as an SRM machine. (SRM stands for Schoberer Resistance Measurement.) The machine takes measurements from the bike's **cranks** and wheels, as well as monitors worn by the cyclist. These produce a figure measuring the cyclist's power output in watts.

Power-to-weight ratios

Cyclists can use SRM testing to find their ideal racing weight. Dividing a cyclist's power output in watts by their weight in kilograms gives a power-to-weight ratio. Cross-country racers aim for as high a power-to-weight ratio as possible.

For example, a cyclist who weighs 65 kilograms but can put out the same power as one who weighs 70 kilograms will be able to ride faster. He has to move less weight using the same power. But if he loses weight he may no longer be able to generate the same power. SRM machines help cyclists tailor their training and food intake to get the best possible power-to-weight ratio.

Heavy training versus racing

During the racing season most riders maintain their fitness through light workouts. The racing itself pushes their bodies to the limit, so training is geared to keeping **aerobic** fitness and recovering from the effects of racing. During the **off-season**, riders put in periods of extremely hard training in order to build their fitness and strength.

Road riding and cyclo-cross

Many mountain bikers use road bikes as part of their training. They can cover more kilometres per hour than on a mountain bike, getting crucial fitness into their legs. Riders like Barrie Clarke, one of Britain's top mountain-bike racers, also use running, swimming and **cyclo-cross** to vary winter training.

Running is good for leg strength and overall fitness, so many top riders use running as a way of varying their training programme.

Britain's Jenny Copnall stretches before a race, so that her muscles will be relaxed and ready to work. Racing or training with tense muscles can lead to injury.

Stretching and flexibility

Throughout periods of heavy training it is important for racers to keep muscles flexible. Flexibility describes the range of movement each muscle can work through. Having good flexibility allows an off-road racer to apply power from unexpected positions – often helpful on a bumpy mountain-bike course.

Cyclo-cross fact

Cyclo-cross is a cross between road racing and mountain biking. Competitions are held on an off-road course using modified road bikes with drop handlebars. Riders often have to carry their bikes over obstacles or up steep slopes.

Eating for fitness

Food is a crucial part of any cyclist's training. On a basic level, if they do not eat enough, they 'bonk' – a cycling expression that means 'run out of energy'! But racers also take advice from **nutritionists** on exactly what they should eat, how much and when to eat it. These are all crucial markers on the road to winning.

Different food types

Top-level racers, such as the 2000 world champion Marga Fullana of Spain, combine different foods in a very specific way. About 60–65 per cent of their **calories** come from carbohydrates. The body converts carbohydrates into glucose for energy, and stores reserve glucose as glycogen.

About 20–25 per cent of a top rider's food should be made up of fats, though this would be a high percentage for a 'normal' person. Fat is an important energy source, and as the body runs out of glycogen it uses fatty acids as an energy source instead. Fat is also a crucial part of nerve fibres and helps regulate the body's temperature.

The last 10–15 per cent of their diet should be made up of protein, such as lean meat or chicken. Proteins help the body to grow, maintain and repair itself.

Getting enough fuel on board is crucial for riders if they are to train and race well. Otherwise they may 'bonk' – run out of energy in the middle of a ride.

Carbo fact

There are two different types of carbohydrate, simple and complex. Simple carbohydrates such as sugar are absorbed quickly by the body. Complex carbohydrates such as pasta and bread are absorbed more slowly.

Feeding time

Food provides riders with enough energy to go out and train for long hours in the saddle. Most coaches and nutritionists advise riders to eat a good meal before a 2–6 hour training ride. This should include plenty of complex carbohydrates such as bread, pasta, rice, muesli or porridge.

Eating after training is also important. Glycogen is the body's reserve food supply, stored in the liver and muscles. During a tough ride, glycogen gets used up. For the first 30 minutes after exercise, the body opens a 'glycogen window', when it is especially able to replace lost glycogen. Eating carbohydrates and a bit of protein while this window is open helps the body to recover more quickly.

Food fact

A top rider can store up to 2000 calories in their body, but will burn 2500–5000 on a four-hour ride. For any ride longer than an hour, riders need to take food with them to eat on the trail, to top up their energy.

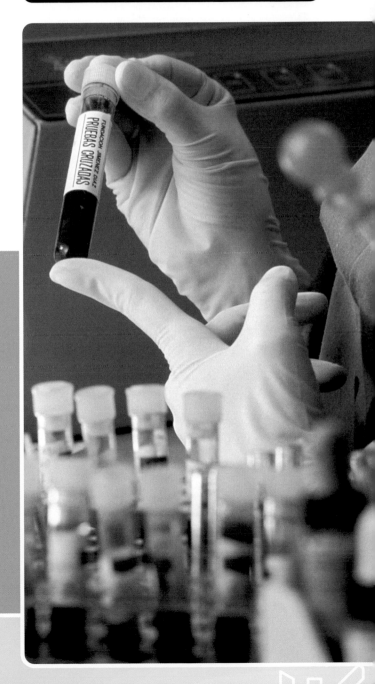

Food supplements and illegal drugs

Many racers take special food supplements like this to help fuel their bodies. They need to be careful about what is in these supplements, however, as some them contain illegal performance-enhancing drugs.

For decades, cycling has been associated with deliberate illegal drug-taking. A high number of top road-racers have died of heart problems, which are often connected to drug abuse. Partly because of this, mountain bikers are now subjected to strict tests both at competitions and during training.

Racing fuel

On one of the mountain stages of the 2003 Tour de France, race favourite Lance Armstrong suddenly began to struggle to keep up. He later explained that he had 'bonked' – run out of energy – and could have lost the whole race through the simple mistake of not eating enough.

Race lead-in

Before the Second World War, racing cyclists thought the best food they could eat was steak – preferably as raw as possible. Today, **nutritionists** understand better how food affects a cyclist. While protein-rich foods like steak are important, today's racers eat a more balanced diet.

Two or three days before a race, most cross-country mountain-bike riders try to make sure they eat plenty of carbohydrates and drink lots of fluid. Typical meals might include a breakfast of cereals, fruit or pasta, then a lunch and dinner of bean stew, pasta or rice, with potatoes, vegetables and meat (usually lean red meat or a white meat such as chicken).

A quick snack during a long race helps keep competitors' energy levels up. Racers practise eating (and drinking from a water bottle) while on the move, so they can manage it easily in races.

Race-day food

About three hours before the start of their race riders eat a 'race breakfast' – something rich in carbohydrate, with extra protein, maybe rice or pasta with an egg on top. They avoid anything too sugary, because the simple carbohydrates in sugar would be broken down too quickly to benefit them in the race.

Intake fact

Top riders live by the rule: 'Eat before you're hungry; drink before you're thirsty.' Taking small amounts of liquid and food regularly helps keep energy levels high.

About 40 minutes before the starting gun, racers eat something like a banana or an energy bar, and drink some sports drink. This makes sure they have some fuel in their stomach at race time. In races of less than an hour, no food needs to be eaten during the actual race itself. But during longer races, riders usually start eating a little food every hour after the first hour has passed.

Vegetarian cyclists

Vegetarian racers, such as 2002 world cross-country champion Gunn-Rita Dahle, are careful to take in plenty of iron in their diet. Iron is an essential part of blood, helping carry oxygen to muscles, and it is lost through heavy sweating. Non-vegetarians get their iron from meat. Vegetarian cyclists get iron from nuts, spinach, broccoli, dried fruit or iron supplements.

Drinks fact

Sports drinks that contain high levels of carbohydrates — needed by cyclists to provide energy — take about 10 minutes to work on the body.

Racers take water on board at a feeding centre during a short road-based leg of a mountain-bike race in the European Alps.

Support crew

Behind most successful racers there is a whole team of people helping them to perform as well as possible. National and professional racing teams have mechanics, team managers, coaches, physiotherapists and sports psychologists to help the riders stay healthy, train better and ultimately win competitions.

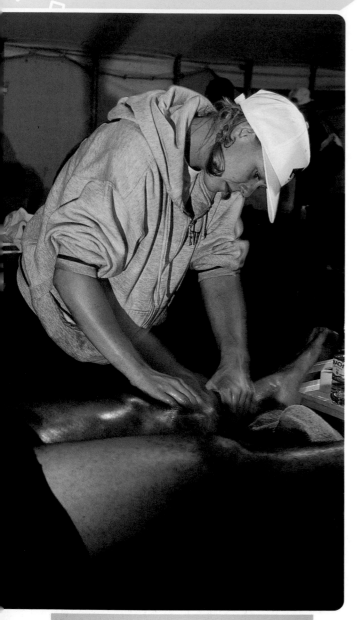

Leg massage after a race or a hard training session can help a rider's muscles recover more quickly than normal. Many top teams have a masseur as part of their support crew.

Team support

Coaches and managers of top-level teams are often ex-racers themselves. Gary Foord, for example, is the coach of the Great Britain cross-country mountain-biking team. In Gary's previous career as a racer he won a World Cup event in California in the USA and raced in the European Championships and the Olympics. People like Gary are able to hand on their experience to younger riders, giving them valuable advice on training, equipment and race tactics.

Physiotherapy and massage

As Gary says, 'In training you have to work on the technical side of things, which is physically demanding but also damaging. Potentially you are going to hurt yourself.' Many teams have a trained physiotherapist on board to help the racers recover from injuries.

Physiotherapists are experts in how the body works. They advise on the best way to maintain fitness while suffering from an injury and may give massage to ease sore muscles. They are most likely to be able to help in cases where injuries have been caused by overtraining or riding in a bad position on the bike.

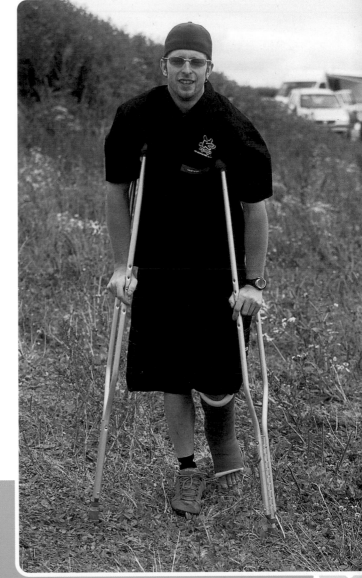

Mechanics are a crucial part of a top mountain biker's support team.

Mental training

Increasingly, top athletes of all kinds take advice from sports psychologists. These are experts in the best mental way to approach training and, especially, competition. They tailor their advice to the particular personality of the racer they are advising – someone with a naturally aggressive racing style, for example, might need to calm down at the start of a race. Someone who is naturally cautious might get advice that helps them to be more aggressive during races.

Scott Beaumont

Nickname: 'Boomboom'
Born: June 1978
Lives: Worcester, England
Honours: BMX World Champion 1995, 1996; British Champion eight times; National Series champion eight times. Biker-X (a bicycle-based, downhill version of **motocross**) champion 1999. Dual: fifth overall, 2000 Dual World Cup.
Current specialities: **BSX**, Dual, **4x**; some downhill racing.

Scott's nickname – 'Boomboom' – is hard-earned, as he has had several serious crashes. Included in these was a terrible crash at the 2002 4x event at Telluride, USA, in which he broke several different leg bones. Despite this he managed to finish twentieth overall in the World Cup standings.

The biking year

Top riders' lives are geared around the racing season. Athens 2004 Olympic competitors like Britain's Liam Killeen began planning for their race early in 2003. Their training, the events they entered, their holidays – in fact, their whole lives – were focused on those few circuits of the Olympic course. This is because it is crucial for riders to plan and time their training so that they reach their peak for important competitions.

Base conditioning

The mountain-bike racing season usually takes place through the late spring, summer and early autumn. In winter, the riders can put in heavy training, because they are unlikely to have a big race coming up. They work on their base conditioning – the basic strength and fitness that will hopefully allow them to win come race time. Their bodies are pushed to the limit. They may use weights (see page 23), and a variety of other training techniques to get them into good basic shape for the next season.

Building to a peak

As the racing season begins, the riders start to cut back the intensity of their training. They stop using weights, and focus more on the bike techniques and skills that will help them win races. Their workouts on the bike begin to be more concerned with speed and less with distance. This is to prepare their bodies for the rapid acceleration and high pace of racing. It also gives their muscles a chance to recover from the hard work done during the months of tough training that have gone before.

Liam Killeen, one of Britain's top racers, has a pre-race chat with Dave Brailsford of the British Cycling Federation. The advice of coaches and managers is crucial in helping riders to reach a peak at exactly the right time.

The final countdown

Leading up to a big race such as the World Championships or Olympics, most riders cut down on their training still further. They know they are fit and they know their techniques are good. Their aim now is to get to the start line in the best condition possible. Light training, with a few sprints thrown in, is combined with eating well, drinking lots of fluid and getting early nights with plenty of sleep. The riders aim to bring their bodies to peak condition on the day of the race.

This is what a whole year's training often boils down to: crossing the finish line ahead of the others.

Alison Dunlap

Height: 168 cm
Weight: 56 kg
Born: July 1969
Hometown: Denver, Colorado, USA
Residence: Colorado Springs, Colorado, USA
Hobbies: Rock climbing, playing the flute and telemark skiing

Career highlights:
- UCI Tissot Mountain Bike World Cup Champion 2002
- UCI Mountain Bike World Champion 2001
- Twice Olympic team member: 2000 mountain bike (seventh), 1996 road race
- National cross-country champion 1999, 2002; short-track cross-country champion 1999, 2002; **cyclo-cross** champion 1997–2001, 2003

Originally a road-racer, Alison won a stage of the Grand Boucle Feminine (the women's Tour de France) in 1996, the first by an American since 1989. She turned to pro-mountain biking in 1997. Alison won the NORBA National Championship and UCI World Cup Overall Championship in 2002 while competing with a broken wrist.

Race preparation

All the years of training a rider does can be wasted if they fail to get themselves ready properly on the day of the race. Each rider knows that every little detail has to be checked. It's a safe bet that their opponents will be making these last-minute checks. Failing to make them yourself might give the opposition a big advantage.

Rider preparation

Riders like former world number one Bart Brentjens of the Netherlands time their training schedule to make sure they reach race day in top shape. On the actual day of a race, they have a ride to get warmed up and do some stretching to keep relaxed. Several hours before the race they eat a race breakfast (see page 30). For an event like the Olympic cross-country in Sydney 2000, which lasted a couple of hours during warm weather, they make sure they are **hydrated** and have some energy snacks with them.

Equipment preparation

National and professional teams have mechanics to check over bikes to make sure they are running smoothly and are undamaged. That way there is less chance of a snapped chain or broken brake cable ruining an important race. Mechanics take their work extremely seriously: Lance Armstrong's mechanic on the Tour de France road race used to sleep with Lance's bike next to his bed, just to make sure that no one else was able to touch it!

The mechanic of UK rider Steve Peat checks over his bike just ahead of a big race. All top riders have a mechanic to set the bike up and make sure it runs smoothly.

Bike check facts

Most amateur riders have to do their own bike checks before a race. They check that:

- there are no frayed cables that could snap
- brake blocks have plenty of wear on them and are about 2 mm from the **rims**

- the **derailleurs** (front and rear) are shifting to all gears properly
- the saddle and seat post are secure
- the headset, handlebars and brake levers are secure
- the wheels are tightened and the quick releases are on.

Coaching and tactics

Before a big race, riders get advice from their coach on the race ahead. This might include suggestions for good spots to launch an attack, how to **pace** the race, and so on. For instance, if a course has a steep uphill section, riders typically keep the pace high along these sections to make sure no one gets ahead of the pack. When they get to the top, the pack relaxes momentarily. A sudden, fierce attack here can allow a rider to take the lead over his or her rivals.

Coaches can also give advice on the technical details of the course: these could include the fastest areas of a long straight or the smoothest line through a downhill section, for example.

Roland Green of Canada, the 2002 cross-country world champion, gets some last-minute advice from his coach before the start of a race.

Racing tactics

Even the best-laid plans can go wrong during a race. The riders who can adapt their tactics to changes in the race are usually the ones who come out on top. The story of the women's cross-country race at the 2003 World Championships in Lugano, Switzerland, shows the changes that can affect the outcome of a race.

Leaders emerge

As the riders began to gather at the start line of the women's cross-country race, the clear favourite was Gunn-Rita Dahle of Norway. Not only was she the current world champion, Gunn-Rita had also won every World Cup race that season. But early in the race she suffered a bad puncture, which allowed the other lead riders a sniff of victory. By halfway through the six-lap, 37-kilometre course, two riders were ahead of the chasing pack: Alison Sydor of Canada and Marga Fullana of Spain.

Tactics facts

When two riders find themselves ahead of the others in a race, they have a choice about how to play things. One sometimes decides to ride on the back wheel of the other, effectively getting a 'tow' from the rider who leads. Or they can work together, sharing the strain at the front. This gives them a better chance of staying ahead of the rest.

Competitors race away from the start of the 2003 world championship women's cross-country. But who would make it across the finishing line first?

Working together

Alison Sydor had won three world championships in a row in 1994, 1995 and 1996, and was desperate to win another. She and Fullana decided to ride together for a while. They took turns leading, pushing the **pace** to try to build up a good gap on the other riders. Then Fullana's bike began to develop mechanical problems and she fell away. Behind, Sabine Spitz of Germany launched a fierce attack, which took her past Fullana and up to Sydor by the end of lap 5, with only one lap to go.

Race to the line

Spitz attacked again, and opened a small gap. She piled on the pressure and the gap steadily grew. By the time they reached the finish, Spitz was ahead – but only just. She crossed the finishing line first, with Sydor missing out on a fourth world championship gold medal by just 16 seconds.

Sabine Spitz celebrates her surprise victory in the 2003 world championship cross-country race. Her late attack took former champion Alison Sydor by surprise.

Big competitions

Cycling's biggest competitions are those approved by the UCI (which stands for Union Cycliste Internationale, or International Cycling Union). The UCI is based in Switzerland, and is the world governing body for all kinds of cycling. Road, BMX, mountain biking and track racing all fall under its control.

Women's downhill racers celebrate on the winner's podium at a round of the World Cup held near Fort William, Scotland.

The World Cup

The World Cup is a series of events held around the world, at which the top riders compete for prize money and World Cup points. The World Cup features downhill and cross-country racing, as well as **4x**. At the end of each season each rider's points total is added up and the winner crowned. The champion for that year has a good claim to being the world's best rider, as they have performed best over a whole year's racing, rather than in a one-off event that happens on a single day.

World Championships

Held every year, the 'Worlds', as most riders call them, are second only to the Olympics in a mountain-bike racer's mind. The racing includes cross-country, downhill and 4x. The format is a one-off competition, where the winner takes all.

Speciality events facts

As well as UCI events, there are special competitions held around the world, usually for TV or video companies to release later. One example of these is the '**freeride**' events **sponsored** by a big energy-drink manufacturer. Top downhill riders compete to perform the most spectacular aerials and manoeuvres on a pre-set course or series of jumps.

The Olympics

Since 1996, every four years the chance has come along to win the biggest prize of all: an Olympic gold medal. But only cross-country riders get the opportunity, as downhill and the other mountain-bike competitions do not feature in the Olympics. For many riders, four years or more of preparation boil down into this couple of hours out on the course.

Alison Dunlap of the USA, the 2001 world cross-country champion, has one dream above all others. She says, 'My big goal of my cycling career was always to win the Olympics. That's something that I'm focusing on and aiming towards.'

Paola Pezzo

Born:	January 1969, Italy
Height:	178 cm
Weight:	62 kg
Lives:	Boscochiesanuova, Italy
Other sports:	Skiing, running
Favourite riders:	Fausto Coppi and Miguel Indurain (both road racers)
Most cherished possession:	Mountain bike

Paola Pezzo is the most successful Olympic mountain biker ever. In 1996 she became the Olympic cross-country mountain bike champion. Then, in 2000, she beat a top-class field to take a second Olympic gold. Paola's favourite colour? 'Gold'!

Pro rider

The lifestyle of pro riders – professional mountain bikers – sounds very glamorous. They get to travel around the world, mixing with other young people who are into the same sport. New bikes are always available, plus other equipment and clothing. Most bikers love their chosen career, but it is not always easy.

Travel

One of the big pluses of being a pro biker is getting the chance to travel. Top riders like downhill maestro Cedric Gracia of Spain get to visit all the world's top venues, and ride them in small groups or alone. The downside to all this travelling is that pro riders are away from home for long periods without seeing their family and friends. They live out of a kitbag and they have to put up with the frustrations of international travel: airlines that do not want to take bikes, delayed flights and bad accommodation.

Bike development

Many riders are involved in helping develop bikes and other equipment for the companies that employ them. They are expected to provide feedback on the geometry (angles and shapes) of the bikes they ride, how they handle, and whether the suspension and brakes work well. Often a bike company's top models are near-direct copies of the machines their racers use. Some racers even have their name attached to a particular model of bike.

'How did this fit in last time?' Packing up bikes for travel is one of the downsides of international mountain bike racing.

Working with sponsors

Non-bike companies sometimes **sponsor** mountain bikers. For example, a car company that makes off-road vehicles might want to be associated with a world champion off-road rider. The riders are given payments or goods – for example, a car – in return for doing publicity work. However, arranging sponsors and financial support can be a tricky job even for top riders. This is especially true in cross-country, which is less appealing to TV audiences than downhill and **4x**, and so has found it increasingly hard to attract sponsors.

Job satisfaction

Despite the difficulties involved, pro mountain bikers are the envy of their friends. The excitement and adventure of their lifestyle are things that none of them would swap for another job. And there's always the chance that one day they may become a champion!

Eric Carter of the USA clatters his way down the course of one of the 2003 World Cup downhill competitions. It takes years of hard training to become a top-level mountain biker like this.

Brian Lopes

Height:	175 cm
Weight:	72 kg
Born:	September 1971
Hobbies:	Wakeboarding, dirt-bike riding, weight training, snorkelling, basketball, music.
Career highlights:	1998: World Championships Dual Slalom Champion; NORBA National Downhill Champion
	1999: NORBA National Dual Slalom Champion
	2000: UCI World Cup Dual Champion – won seven out of eight UCI World Cup Dual races

A pro BMX rider for 11 years and a pro-mountain biker for 9 years, California's Brian Lopes is one of the most successful North American racers ever.

World and Olympic champions

Top mountain bikers face tough competition for medals and championships. Even making the top ten in a race requires a rider to be incredibly fit and a brilliant biker. So when you see names like Filip Meirhaeghe of Belgium or Alison Sydor of Canada appear over and over again, you know they are really world-class performers at the top of their sport!

2003 World Cup

Cross-country, women	
1 Gunn-Rita Dahle (NORWAY)	1250 points
2 Sabine Spitz (GERMANY)	875 points
3 Irina Kalentieva (RUSSIA)	715 points

Cross-country, men	
1 Julien Absalon (FRANCE)	930 points
2 Christoph Sauser (SWITZERLAND)	845 points
3 Filip Meirhaeghe (BELGIUM)	693 points

Downhill, women	
1 Sabrina Jonnier (FRANCE)	834 points
2 Fionn Griffiths (GREAT BRITAIN)	814 points
3 Tracy Moseley (GREAT BRITAIN)	770 points

Downhill, men	
1 Nathan Rennie (AUSTRALIA)	701 points
2 Cedric Gracia (FRANCE)	661 points
3 Mickael Pascal (FRANCE)	656 points

2003 World Champions, Lugano, Switzerland

Elite women's downhill
1 Anne-Caroline Chausson (FRANCE)
2 Sabrina Jonnier (FRANCE)
3 Nolvenn Le Caer (FRANCE)

Elite women's cross-country
1 Sabine Spitz (GERMANY)
2 Alison Sydor (CANADA)
3 Irina Kalentieva (RUSSIA)

Elite men's downhill
1 Greg Minnaar (SOUTH AFRICA)
2 Mickael Pascal (FRANCE)
3 Fabien Barel (FRANCE)

Elite men's cross-country
1 Filip Meirhaeghe (BELGIUM)
2 Ryder Hesjedal (CANADA)
3 Roel Paulissen (BELGIUM)

2000 Olympic medallists, Sydney, Australia

Women	
1 Paola Pezzo (ITALY)	1:49:24.38
2 Barbara Blatter (SWITZERLAND)	1:49:51.42
3 Margarita Fullana (SPAIN)	1:49:57.39

Men	
1 Miguel Martinez (FRANCE)	2:09:02
2 Filip Meirhaeghe (BELGIUM)	2:10:05
3 Christoph Sauser (SWITZERLAND)	2:11:20

1996 Olympic medallists, Atlanta, USA

Women	
1 Paola Pezzo (ITALY)	1:50:51
2 Alison Sydor (CANADA)	1:51:58
3 Susan Demattei (USA)	1:52:36

Men	
1 Bart Jan Brentjens (NETHERLANDS)	2:17:38
2 Thomas Frischknecht (SWITZERLAND)	2:20:14
3 Miguel Martinez (FRANCE)	2:20:36

Glossary

4x
event in which four riders race down a course side by side

aerobic
relating to the amount of oxygen used by the body in exercise

aerobic capacity
the maximum level of exercise at which the body can get enough oxygen to work without using too much

aerodynamic
capable of avoiding wind resistance

axle
pin around which a wheel turns

beach cruiser
an old-fashioned, American style of bike with wide handlebars and fat tyres

body armour
protective clothing worn by people who take part in extreme sports

BSX
short for Bicycle Supercross, a kind of indoor BMX

calories
the units of energy supplied by food

chainset
the cranks and cogs at the front of a bike's drivetrain

cleat
device for attaching a cycle shoe to a pedal

cogs
also called the freewheel, this usually refers to the block of toothed circles of metal at the back of a bike's drivetrain

crank
the 'arm' between the pedal and the bike

cyclo-cross
a sport that mixes cross-country cycling with road-based bicycles

derailleur
the hinged device next to the rear wheel, which allows a cyclist to change gear

drive train
the pedals, cranks, chain and gears of a bike

freeride
riding without boundaries, using tricks and skills to cover difficult ground and obstacles

full-face helmet
a helmet with a section that comes around the chin to protect it

gravity
a force that attracts all objects to one another. The Earth has a gravity that pulls us towards it.

hydrated
with an adequate amount of water

lactate threshold
the point at which the body starts to generate lactic acid in its muscles, as a result of going without enough oxygen

motocross
a motorbike sport where competitors race across a series of obstacles on a circular track

nutrients
parts of food that are needed by living things in order for them to stay alive

nutritionist
an expert who advises people on the best, healthiest foods for them to eat

off-season
period when riders concentrate on training instead of competitions

pace
the speed at which something is done

plumb line
a weighted piece of string, which dangles straight downwards

rims
the outer part of the wheel, to which the spokes are attached. Tyres go on to the outside of the rims.

spokes
the thin metal rods that join the hub (centre) of the wheel to the rim

sponsor
someone who gives money or other support to help an activity take place

Resources

Further reading

To The Limit: Mountain Biking, Paul Mason (Hodder Wayland, 2000)
Written specifically for young people, this book covers the basics of mountain biking.

Mountain Bike Fitness Training, John Metcalfe (Mainstream Publishing, 2001)
This book provides information about fitness training for mountain bikers.

Zinn and the Art of Mountain Bike Maintenance, Lennard Zinn (Velo Press, 2001)
The standard reference book for home bike mechanics.

Mountain Bike Like a Champion: Master All the Skills to Tackle the Toughest Terrain, Ned Overend, Ed Pavelka (Rodale Press, 1999)
Helpful guidance from Ned Overend, one of the USA's most successful and experienced mountain bike pro riders.

Dirt! The Philosophy, Technique & Practice of Mountain Biking, John Howard (The Lyons Press, 1997)
Offers details of lots of techniques for all aspects of mountain biking.

Useful websites and addresses

USA Cycling
1 Olympic Plaza
Colorado Springs, CO 80909
USA
www.usacycling.org/mtb

MTBA (Mountain Bike Australia)
PO Box 4604
Kingston ACT 2604
Australia
www.mtba.asn.au

New Zealand Mountain Bike Web
There is a website for New Zealand-based mountain bikers at
www.mountainbike.co.nz

British Cycling
National Cycling Centre
Stuart Street
Manchester
M11 4DQ
www.bcf.uk.com

Disclaimer

All the Internet addresses (URLs) given in this book were valid at the time of going to press. However, due to the dynamic nature of the Internet, some addresses may have changed, or sites may have changed or ceased to exist since publication. While the author and Publishers regret any inconvenience this may cause readers, no responsibility for any such changes can be accepted by either the author or the Publishers.

Index

aerodynamics 13, 16, 17

beach cruisers 6, 8
Beaumont, Scott 33
bike checks 36, 37
bike development 42
bike set-up 12, 16–17
bike types 12–13
body armour 7, 15
'bonk' (running out of energy) 28, 30
brakes 13, 37

cadence 18, 19
carbohydrates 28, 29, 30, 31
Chausson, Anne-Caroline 4, 5, 44
Clarke, Barrie 24, 27
cleats 13, 17
clothing 8, 14, 15
clubs 10
coaches 32, 10, 37
cross-country racing 6, 12, 13, 22, 26, 40, 41, 43
cross training 23, 26–7
cyclo-cross 27

Dahle, Gunn-Rita 19, 31, 38, 44
diet and nutrition 28–31, 36
downhill racing 4–5, 7, 12, 13, 15, 20, 21, 40
dual slalom 6, 12
Dunlap, Alison 12, 35, 41

endurance races 7, 22
endurance and strength 22–3, 34
equipment 8, 14–15
escape routes 9

fitness 22–3, 24, 26, 27, 34
flexibility 22, 27
food supplements 29
Foord, Gary 32
4x racing 6, 40
frames 12, 16
freeride events 40
Frischknecht, Thomas 7, 45
front suspension 13

gears 8, 18, 19
glycogen 28, 29
Green, Roland 11
groupset 13

handlebars 13, 17
hazard fixation 20
heart rate 24, 25
helmets 7, 15
hydration 15, 30, 31, 36

injuries 27, 32, 33
International Cycling Union 40
iron 31

Juarez, Tinker 21

Killeen, Liam 34

Lopes, Brian 23, 43

massage 7, 32
mechanics 7, 36
Meirhaeghe, Filip 16, 44
mental training 33

obstacles 20
off-season 23, 27
Olympic medallists 45
Olympics 14, 35, 41
overtraining 25, 32

Peat, Steve 20, 36
pedals 13, 17
Pezzo, Paola 41, 45
physiotherapists 32
picking a line 20
power-to-weight ratios 26
professional mountain bikers 42–3
punctures 9, 15

race preparation 36–7
racing season 34–5
riding style 18–19
road riding 27

saddles 12, 13, 17
safety gear 15
Sauser, Christof 18, 44
Spitz, Sabine 39, 44
sponsors and financial support 10, 40, 43
sports drinks 31
SRM machines 26
starting to race 8–9, 10–11
summer biking gear 14
Sydor, Alison 37, 38, 39, 45

talent scouts 11
team support 32–3
technique 18, 19, 20–1, 37, 38, 41
Thomas, Sue 10
tool kit 15
'tow' 38
training 23, 24–7, 32, 34, 35
turns 20, 21
tyres 8, 9, 12

uphill technique 18, 19, 20, 37, 41

vanishing point 21

weight, balancing 21
weight training 23, 34
wheels 12, 37
winter biking gear 14
world champions 44
World Championships 4–5, 35, 38–9, 40
World Cup 40

young riders 11